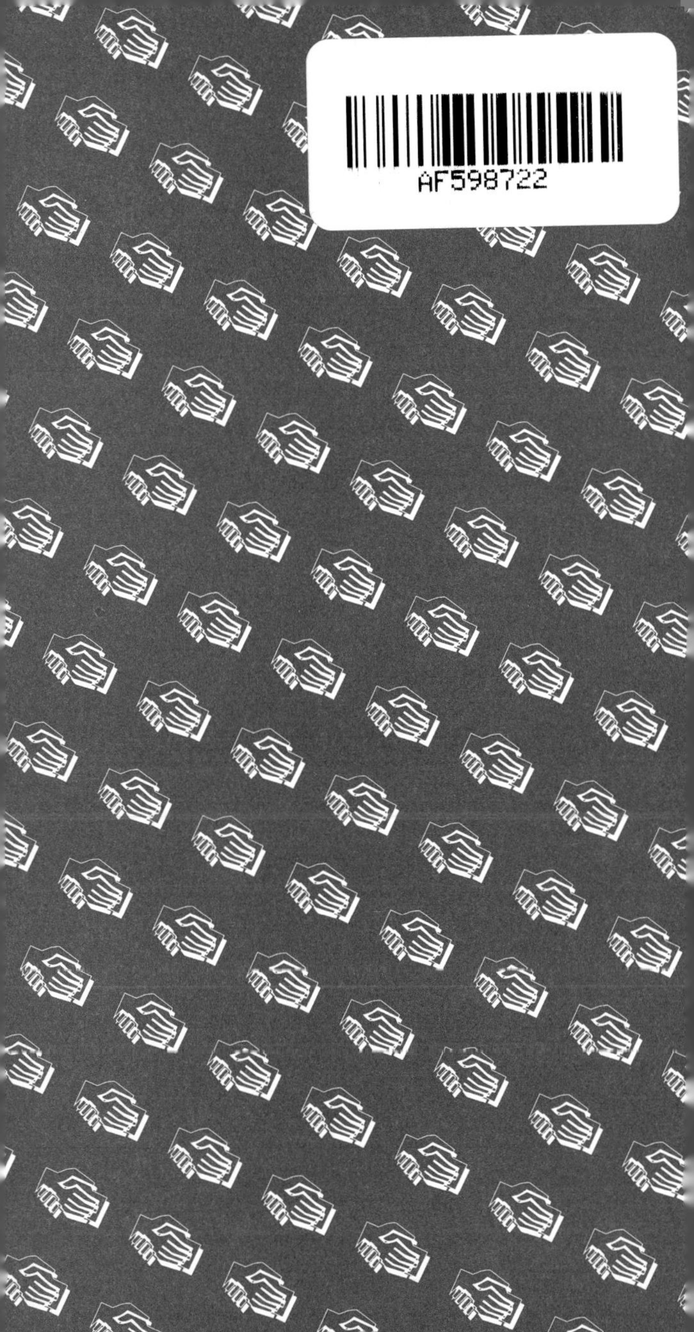
AF598722

The Power of Partnership

Quotations on Relationships & Results

Applewood Books
Bedford, Massachusetts

This book has been prepared by Applewood Books, Inc.

Thank you for purchasing an Applewood Book. Applewood reprints America's lively classics—books from the past that are still of interest to modern readers. For a free copy of our current catalog, please write to Applewood Books, P.O. Box 365, Bedford, MA 01730.

ISBN 1-55709-945-6

10 9 8 7 6 5 4 3 2

Publisher's Note

The connection we have with one another— bonds of family, business, political or religious affiliation, or just about any other common interest—is the chemistry that holds society together. Only when bonds develop between us can we collaborate and work toward a common goal; otherwise we remain isolated individuals. This is the power of partnership and its applications at work, school, and home are endless.

When researching the quotations for this collection, the eighth in our Quote/Unquote series, we sought the wisdom of thoughtful people in many areas of endeavor, including business leaders, statesmen, journalists, academics, and artists. We looked for insights into relationships between individuals and among individuals and organizations. We wanted to illustrate through the words of those who have achieved success in diverse fields why these relationships are so important and how it is that they enhance our ability to achieve our goals.

We hope you will find in these pages insight, humor, warmth and especially the motivation to reach out and forge the new partnerships that will enable you to accomplish your goals and to connect with others to make your dreams come true.

Relationships

Treasure your relationships, not your possessions.

ANTHONY D'ANGELO

Alone we can do so little; together we can do so much.

HELEN KELLER

Everything starts with the customer.

LOUIS V. GERSTNER, JR.

Do good to your friends to keep them, to your enemies to win them.

Benjamin Franklin

Treat people as if they were what they ought to be and you help them to become what they are capable of being.

Johann Wolfgang von Goethe

Think like a wise man but communicate in the language of the people.

William Butler Yeats

I present myself to you in a form suitable to the relationship I wish to achieve with you.

LUIGI PIRANDELLO

Relationships of trust depend on our willingness to look not only to our own interests, but also the interests of others.

PETER FARQUHARSON

All business success rests on something labeled a sale, which at least momentarily weds company and customer.

TOM PETERS

No individual builds anything worthwhile by his efforts alone.

Lloyd Noble

Trust is the lubrication that makes it possible for organizations to work.

Warren Bennis

Motivate employees, train employees, care about employees, and make winners out of employees . . . they'll treat the customers right. And if customers are treated right, they'll come back.

John W. Marriott, Jr.

The gap separating mediocre and outstanding service/quality performers is often widest in the amount and frequency of customer listening.

JIM CLEMMER

Don't walk behind me, I may not lead. Don't walk in front of me, I may not follow. Just walk beside me and be my friend.

ALBERT CAMUS

If you make a sale, you can make a living. If you make an investment of time and good service in a customer, you can make a fortune.

JIM ROHN

I don't wish to be everything to everyone, but I would like to be something to someone.

JAVAN

You'll never get the best from employees by trying to build a fire under them—you've got to build a fire within them.

BOB NELSON

Electric communication will never be a substitute for the face of someone who with their soul encourages another person to be brave and true.

CHARLES DICKENS

The highest compact we can make with our fellow is, "Let there be truth between us two forevermore."

RALPH WALDO EMERSON

To excel forward in a relationship, a situation, and most importantly life, one must first forget about the past.

REGINA MCKAY

The biggest mistake is believing there is one right way to listen, to talk, to have a conversation—or a relationship.

DEBORAH TANNEN

As we look ahead into the next century, leaders will be those who empower others.

BILL GATES

Cherish your human connections—your relationships with friends and family.

BARBARA BUSH

We cannot live only for ourselves. A thousand fibers connect us with our fellow-men; and along those fibers, as sympathetic threads, our actions run as causes, and they come back to us as effects.

HERMAN MELVILLE

There is great comfort and inspiration in the feeling of close human relationships and its bearing on our mutual fortunes.

WALT DISNEY

It seems essential, in relationships and all tasks, that we concentrate only on what is most significant and important.

SOREN KIERKEGAARD

All for one, one for all.

ALEXANDRE DUMAS

If civilization is to survive, we must cultivate the science of human relationships.

FRANKLIN D. ROOSEVELT

A relationship has a momentum, it must change and develop, and will tend to move toward the point of greatest commitment.

CAROLYN HEILBRUN

Always do what you say you are going to do. It is the glue and fiber that binds successful relationships.

JEFFREY A. TIMMONS

If you wish others to believe in you, you must first convince them that you believe in them.

HARVEY MCKAY

We control fifty percent of a relationship. We influence one hundred percent of it.

BARBARA COLOROSE

A relationship needs balance, not complete equality in everything.

HOWARD J. RANKIN

People do not want to be sold a product or service. They want to deal with people who they think have their interest or who care about them.

J. Oliver Crom

Rule No. 1—The customer is always right. Rule No. 2—If the customer is ever wrong, re-read Rule No. 1.

Stew Leonard

We live at a moment when our relationships to each other, and to all other beings with whom we share this planet, are up for grabs.

Carl Sagan

Provision for others is a fundamental responsibility of human life.

WOODROW T. WILSON

All people smile in the same language.

SOURCE UNKNOWN

Just the act of listening means more than you can imagine to most employees.

BOB NELSON

Be everywhere, do everything, and never fail to astonish the customer.

MACY'S MOTTO

Without relationships, no matter how much wealth, fame power, prestige and seeming success by the standards and opinions of thc world one has, happiness will constantly elude him.

SIDNEY MADWED

Assumptions are the termites of relationships.

HENRY WINKLER

When you make a commitment to a relationship, you invest your attention and energy in it more profoundly because you now experience ownership of that relationship.

BARBARA DE ANGELIS

A relationship, I think is like a shark, you know? It has to constantly move forward or it dies. And I think what we got on our hands is a dead shark.

WOODY ALLEN

Every relationship that does not raise us up pulls us down, and vice versa.

FRIEDERICH NIETZSCHE

The formula for achieving a successful relationship is simple: you should treat all disasters as if they were trivialities but never treat a triviality as if it were a disaster.

QUENTIN CRISP

The customer isn't king anymore. The customer is dictator.

RETAILER QUOTED IN *FORTUNE*

We have hundreds of thousands of salespeople. They are our customers.

SCOTT COOK

I came with the mind-set of a customer.

LOU V. GERSTNER

Every company has two organizational structures: The formal one is written on the charts; the other is the everyday relationship of the men and women in the organization.

HAROLD S. GENEEN

Human relationships always help us to carry on because they always presuppose further developments, a future. . . .

ALBERT CAMUS

Every business starts with a dream and builds its reality on relationships.

JOHN L. PICARD

Something must happen; that is the reason for most human relationships.

ALBERT CAMUS

History can predict nothing except that great changes in human relationships will never come about in the form in which they have been anticipated.

JOHAN HUIZINGA

The customer is the immediate jewel of our souls. Him we flatter, him we feast, compliment, vote for, and will not contradict.

RALPH WALDO EMERSON

Our greatest opportunities for advancing productivity and improving living standards are to be found in the field of human relationships.

LOUIS RUTHENBURG

Set and live by this ironclad rule—all promises to customers are kept. Period.

JIM CLEMMER

If you really want to make the sale, make your pitch, provide the sales contract, give the decision-maker the pen, and then sit back and shut up!

CHARLES BETTGER

Outstanding leaders go out of their way to boost the self-esteem of their personnel. If people believe in themselves, it's amazing what they can accomplish.

SAM WALTON

Better understated than overstated. Let people be surprised that it was more than you promised and easier than you said.

JIM ROHN

Anything done for another is done for oneself.

Pope Boniface VIII

The greatest good we can do for others is not to share our riches with them, but to reveal their own.

Source Unknown

The person who figures out how to harness the collective genius of his or her organization is going to blow the competition away.

Walter Wriston

The easiest kind of relationship is with ten thousand people, the hardest is with one.

JOAN BAEZ

Leaders continuously ask customers, external partners, and their internal partners how they can harness and improve the organization's core technologies, processes, and systems to meet everyone's needs.

JIM CLEMMER

Our best thoughts come from others.

RALPH WALDO EMERSON

Trust men and they will be true to you; treat them greatly and they will show themselves great.

Ralph Waldo Emerson

No employer today is independent of those about him. He cannot succeed alone, no matter how great his ability or capital. Business today is more than ever a question of cooperation.

Orison Swett Marden

You don't develop courage by being happy in your relationships everyday. You develop it by surviving difficult times and challenging adversity.

Barbara De Angelis

It is one of the most beautiful compensations of this life that no man can sincerely try to help another without helping himself.

RALPH WALDO EMERSON

The growth and development of people is the highest calling of leadership.

HARVEY S. FIRESTONE

It's the pack that gets the job done, not the lone wolf.

MIKE O'NEIL

Results

Big results require big ambitions.

HERACLITUS

When you're committed to something, you accept no excuses, only results.

ART TUROCK

There is no such thing as failure. There are only results.

ANTHONY ROBBINS

Insanity: doing the same thing over and over again and expecting different results.

ALBERT EINSTEIN

Success usually comes to those who are too busy to be looking for it.

HENRY DAVID THOREAU

Results! Why, man, I have gotten a lot of results. I know several thousand things that won't work.

THOMAS EDISON

Don't tell people how to do things. Tell them what to do and let them surprise you with their results.

George S. Patton

You ask me why I do not write something. . . I think one's feelings waste themselves in words, they ought to be distilled into actions and into actions which bring results.

Florence Nightingale

Competition is a painful thing, but it produces great result.

Jerry Flint

Once you replace negative thoughts with positive ones, you'll start having positive results.

WILLIE NELSON

You are today where your thoughts have brought you; you will be tomorrow where your thoughts take you. You cannot escape the results of your thoughts.

AUTHOR UNKNOWN

Those who trust to chance must abide by the results of chance.

CALVIN COOLIDGE

Let us watch well our beginnings and results will manage themselves.

ALEXANDER CLARK

In all human affairs there are efforts, and there are results, and the strength of effort is the measure of results.

JAMES ALLEN

The reward of a thing well done is to have done it.

RALPH WALDO EMERSON

If at first you don't succeed, try, and try again. Then give up. There's no sense in being a damned fool about it.

W.C. Fields

Honestly achieved results surpass all others.

Michael Diamond

The study and knowledge of the universe would somehow be lame and defective were no practical results to follow.

Marcus Tullius Cicero

I've always believed that if you put in the work, the results will come. I don't do things half-heartedly. Because I know if I do then I can expect half-hearted results.

MICHAEL JORDAN

Only by great risks can great results be achieved.

XERXES

People love chopping wood. In this activity one immediately sees results.

ALBERT EINSTEIN

One's objective should be to get it right, get it quick, get it out and get it over.

WARREN BUFFET

Act, look, feel successful, conduct yourself accordingly, and you will be amazed at the positive results.

WILLIAM JAMES

However beautiful the strategy, you should occasionally look at the results.

SIR WINSTON CHURCHILL

The engine of success is fueled by the "Power of Partnership."

JOHN L. PICARD

The man who gets the most satisfactory results is not always the man with the brilliant single mind, but rather the man who can best co-ordinate the brains and talents of his associates.

W. ALTON JONES

Everyone ought to bear patiently the results of his own conduct.

WILLIAM SHAKESPEARE

You may never know what results come from your action. But if you do nothing, there will be no result.

MAHATMA GANDHI

Managers in all too many American companies do not achieve the desired results because nobody makes them do it.

HAROLD GENEEN

Concentration is the factor that causes the great discrepancy between men and the results they achieve.

ORISON SWETT MARDEN

A pat on the back, though only a few vertebrae removed from a kick in the pants, is miles ahead in results.

BENNETT CERF

Getting results through people is a skill that cannot be learned in the classroom.

J. PAUL GETTY

Only when genius is married to science, can the biggest results be produced.

HERBERT SPENCER

Regardless of how you feel inside, always try to look like a winner. Even if you are behind, a sustained look of control and confidence can give you a mental edge that results in victory.

Arthur Ashe

The genius of the American system is that we have created extraodinary results from plain old people.

Phil Gramm

Work joyfully and peacefully, knowing that right thoughts and right efforts inevitably bring about right results.

James Allen

Waiting is a trap. There will always be reasons to wait. The truth is, there are only two things in life, reasons and results, and reasons simply don't count.

ROBERT ANTHONY

We must reinforce arguments with results.

BOOKER T. WASHINGTON

You don't concentrate on risks. You concentrate on results. No risk is too great to prevent the necessary job from getting done.

CHUCK YEAGER

All progress is based upon a universal innate desire on the part of every organism to live beyond its income.

SAMUEL BUTLER

I think that being able to communicate with people is power. One of my main goals on the planet is to encourage people to empower themselves.

OPRAH WINFREY

Success with money, family, relationships, health, and careers is the ability to reach your personal objectives in the shortest time, with the least effort and with the fewest mistakes.

CHARLES GIVENS

When the pursuit of natural harmony is a shared journey, great heights can be attained.

LYNN HILL

If you mean to profit, learn to please.

WINSTON CHURCHILL

Take time to appreciate employees and they will reciprocate in a thousand ways.

BOB NELSON

Who is the happiest of men? He who values the merits of others, and in their pleasure takes joy, even as though t'were his own.

JOHANN WOLFGANG VON GOETHE

I make progress by having people around me who are smarter than I am and listening to them. And I assume that everyone is smarter about something than I am.

HENRY J. KAISER

Selling is a person-to-person business. You cannot send the sales manual out to make the sale. Sales manuals have no legs and no voice.

JIM ROHN

Your most unhappy customers are your greatest source of learning.

BILL GATES

When somebody shares, everybody wins.

JIM ROHN

You have to treat your employees like your customers. When you treat them right, then they will treat your outside customers right.

HERB KELLEHER

You can have everything in life you want if you just help enough other people get what they want.

Zig Ziglar

It is the diversity of our knowledge, experiences, opinions, personalities and spirit that makes us strong. It is the balance that we bring to this team that frees us and enables us to be great! It is each individual's contribution regardless of size, that allows us to achieve anything.

Mike O'Neil

Light is the task where many share the toil.

Homer

You can only govern men by serving them. The rule is without exception.

Victor Cousin

What we have done for ourselves alone dies with us; what we have done for others and the world remains and is immortal.

Albert Pike

Our success has really been based on partnerships from the very beginning.

Bill Gates

We defend and we build a way of life, not for America alone, but for all mankind.

Franklin D. Roosevelt

Man's great power of thinking, remembering, and communicating are responsible for the evolution of civilization.

Linus Pauling

People may take a job for more money, but they often leave it for more recognition.

Bob Nelson

The thing that lies at the foundation of positive change, the way I see it, is service to a fellow human being.

LECH WALESA

Adversity draws men together and produces beauty and harmony in life's relationships, just as the cold of winter produces ice-flowers on the window-panes, which vanish with the warmth.

SOREN KIERKEGAARD

Always bear in mind that your own resolution to succeed is more important than any other.

ABRAHAM LINCOLN

Don't stay in bed, unless you can make money in bed.

GEORGE BURNS

First they ignore you, then they laugh at you, then they fight you, then you win.

MAHATMA GANDHI

Make everything as simple as possible, but not simpler.

ALBERT EINSTEIN

Well done is better than well said.

BENJAMIN FRANKLIN

The more I want to get something done, the less I call it work.

RICHARD BACH

Success is the sum of small efforts, repeated day in and day out.

ROBERT COLLIER

If you're strong enough, there are no precedents.

F. Scott Fitzgerald

I was bold in the pursuit of knowledge, never fearing to follow truth and reason to whatever results they led.

Thomas Jefferson

We won't pay for progress reports. We'll pay for results.

Tom Ehrenfeld

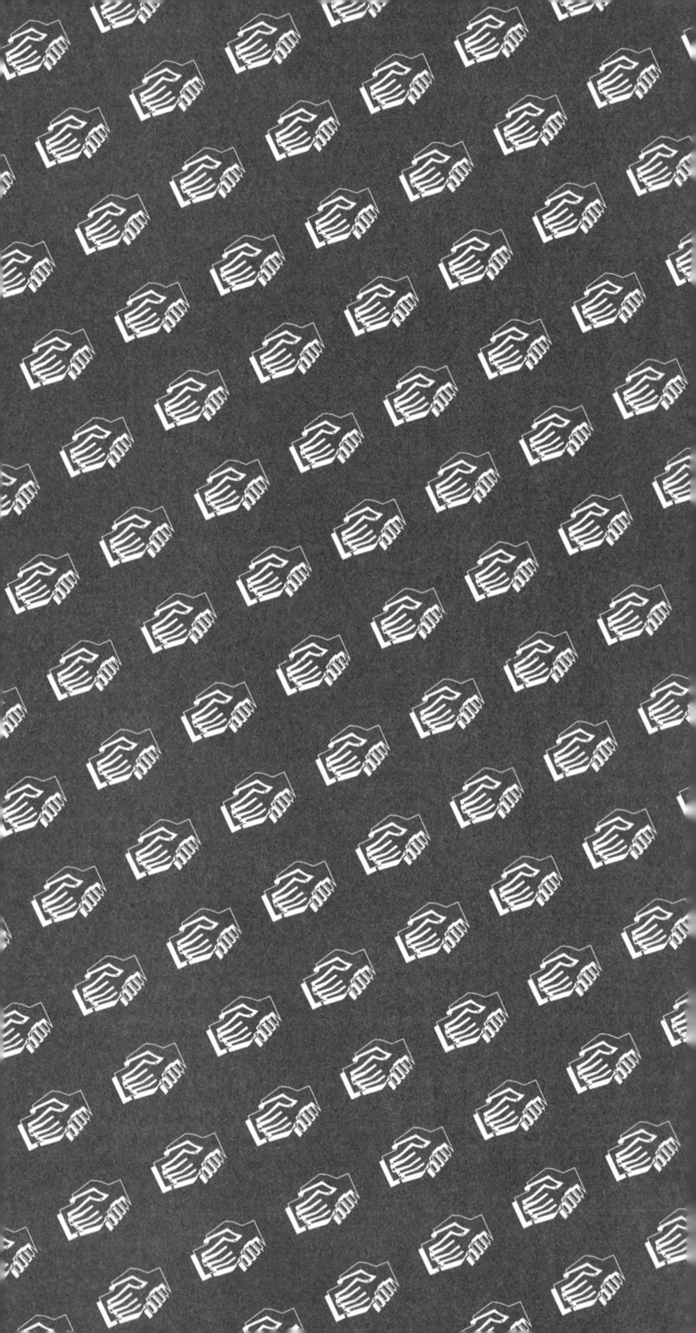